STUDIES IN ECONOMIC

This series, specially commissi_____
Society, provides a guide to the _____
key themes of economic and so_____ _____ advances
have recently been made or in which there has been significant
debate.

Originally entitled 'Studies in Economic History', in 1974 the
series had its scope extended to include topics in social history,
and the new series title, 'Studies in Economic and Social History',
signalises this development.

The series gives readers access to the best work done, helps
them to draw their own conclusions in major fields of study, and
by means of the critical bibliography in each book guides them
in the selection of further reading. The aim is to provide a
springboard to further work rather than a set of pre-packaged
conclusions or short-cuts.

ECONOMIC HISTORY SOCIETY

The Economic History Society, which numbers over 3000
members, publishes the *Economic History Review* four times a year
(free to members) and holds an annual conference. Enquiries
about membership should be addressed to the Assistant Secre-
tary, Economic History Society, Peterhouse, Cambridge. Full-
time students may join the Society at special rates.

STUDIES IN ECONOMIC AND SOCIAL HISTORY

Edited for the Economic History Society by M. W. Flinn and T. C. Smout

PUBLISHED

OTHER TITLES ARE IN PREPARATION

The Myth of the Great Depression, 1873–1896

Prepared for
The Economic History Society by

S. B. SAUL, B.COM., PH.D.

Vice-Chancellor,
University of York

© The Economic History Society 1969

All rights reserved. No part of this publication may be reproduced or transmitted, in any form or by any means, without permission.

First edition 1969
Reprinted (with corrections) 1969, 1972, 1976, 1978

Published by
THE MACMILLAN PRESS LTD
London and Basingstoke
Associated companies in Delhi Dublin
Hong Kong Johannesburg Lagos Melbourne
New York Singapore and Tokyo

ISBN 0 333 04972 1

Printed in Hong Kong

This book is sold subject to the standard conditions of the Net Book Agreement.

The paperback edition of this book is sold subject to the condition that it shall not, by way of trade or otherwise, be lent, resold, hired out, or otherwise circulated without the publisher's prior consent, in any form of binding or cover other than that in which it is published and without a similar condition including this condition being imposed on the subsequent purchaser.

Contents

List of Diagrams and Tables

Acknowledgements

I would like to express my thanks to W. Ashworth, D. J. Coppock, M. W. Flinn, A. E. Musson and T. C. Smout, who all read the manuscript and made most valuable suggestions.

The cover picture comes from the journal *Commerce*, 2 August 1899.

Edinburgh   S. B. S.
May 1968

Preface

SO long as the study of economic history was confined to only a small group at a few universities, its literature was not prolific and its few specialists had no great problem in keeping abreast of the work of their colleagues. Even in the 1930s there were only two journals devoted exclusively to this field. But the high quality of the work of the economic historians during the inter-war period and the post-war growth in the study of the social sciences sparked off an immense expansion in the study of economic history after the Second World War. There was a great expansion of research and many new journals were launched, some specialising in branches of the subject like transport, business or agricultural history. Most significantly, economic history began to be studied as an aspect of history in its own right in schools. As a consequence, the examining boards began to offer papers in economic history at all levels, while textbooks specifically designed for the school market began to be published.

For those engaged in research and writing this period of rapid expansion of economic history studies has been an exciting, if rather breathless one. For the larger numbers, however, labouring in the outfield of the schools and colleges of further education, the excitement of the explosion of research has been tempered by frustration caused by its vast quantity and, frequently, its controversial character. Nor, it must be admitted, has the ability or willingness of the academic economic historians to generalise and summarise marched in step with their enthusiasm for research.

The greatest problems of interpretation and generalisation have tended to gather round a handful of principal themes in economic history. It is, indeed, a tribute to the sound sense of economic historians that they have continued to dedicate their energies, however inconclusively, to the solution of these key problems. The results of this activity, however, much of it stored away in a wide range of academic journals, have tended to remain inaccessible to many of those currently interested in the subject. Recognising the need for guidance through the burgeoning and confusing literature that has grown around these basic topics, the Economic History Society decided to launch this series of small books. The books are intended to serve as guides to current interpretations in important fields of economic history in which important advances have recently been made, or in which there has recently been some significant debate. Each book aims to survey recent work, to indicate the full scope of the particular problem as it has been opened up by recent scholarship, and to draw such conclusions as seem warranted, given the present state of knowledge and understanding. The authors will often be at pains to point out where, in their view, because of a lack of information or inadequate research, they believe it is premature to attempt to draw firm conclusions. While authors will not hesitate to review recent and older work critically, the books are not intended to serve as vehicles for their own specialist views: the aim is to provide a balanced summary rather than an exposition of the author's own viewpoint. Each book will include a descriptive bibliography.

In this way the series aims to give all those interested in economic history at a serious level access to recent scholarship in some major fields. Above all, the aim is to help the reader to draw his own conclusions, and to guide him in the selection of further reading as a means to this end, rather than to present him with a set of pre-packaged conclusions.

University of Edinburgh
June 1968

M. W. FLINN
Editor

The Problem

IN this book we are primarily concerned with finding out how economic historians have been analysing the two decades or so which followed the boom of the early 1870s and ended in the middle of the 1890s, a period which they have characterised as the 'Great Depression'. We shall be asking ourselves three major questions. First of all, what sort of depression are we thinking about; what indicators can we employ and how do they move? Secondly, how do we explain these movements and to what extent are they interconnected? Finally, how far in fact can we justify picking out these years as a period with an economic meaning and unity of their own? Our procedure will be to take various indicators in turn and to look at these problems in terms of each as we go along.

There are several economic series which we might expect to point to a depression, that is to say which might show a decline or move in an unfavourable manner for some interested parties at least. We must be careful to remember that while some series might show an *actual fall* others may show a *fall in their rate of growth*. It is an important distinction and we shall certainly come across both types of movement. Prices, interest rates, production, employment, investment, national income, wages, profits, foreign trade, the terms of trade will all concern us, but we shall concentrate most of all upon prices and industrial production. This is not because these are necessarily the most important elements in economic life but because over the years in question their trends were the most pronounced and have caused most controversy, and because it is reasonable to believe that movements in the other indicators depended heavily upon changes in these two.

Our third question does pose perhaps the most serious difficulties, and it will be useful to indicate their nature now so as to prepare for more detailed discussion later. The last half-century to 1914 has excited the attention of historians because of the belief, which was felt by many at the time, too, that in some way it marks a watershed in British economic history. The industrialisation of other countries, the growing competition in world

9

trade, the sharp adjustments to the pattern of farming, all give the impression of an era of British economic supremacy coming to an end. This may well be, but it is a very different matter from arguing that the years from 1873 to 1896 were in themselves of special significance.

For this to be the case it must be shown that there are trends in that period which are markedly different from those discernible before and afterwards. If we can show this for only one of the indicators it will not be of any great moment, because we can do this for all kinds of indicators at different moments in history. To have substantial significance for our understanding of the progress of the economy as a whole, we must be able to show that several indicators can be seen as operating in a particular way just during those particular years.

An important point to bear in mind is that identification of the 'Great Depression' as a special period derives from the interest of economists and historians in the various swings of economic activity which they see as characterising industrial economies in particular. The pattern is a complex one, for cycles of different lengths have been identified and they overlap to a considerable extent. There is the four-year cycle most prominent in the U.S.A., the eight- to ten-year 'trade cycle' ruling in Britain. Others have seen the British economy from 1870 to 1914 as dominated by twenty-year swings, not of total activity but of home and foreign investment. The concept of the 'Great Depression', however, emerges from analyses made in terms of even longer swings of fifty years' duration. Such an approach divides the nineteenth century into four periods, each half of a long swing. These run from 1815 to the mid-1840s; thence to 1873: the 'Great Depression' years; and finally from 1896 to 1914.

We must say right away that there are grave doubts as to the validity of placing the British economy within the strait jacket of such time periods. It is, after all, difficult to be confident of the reality of such fluctuations when there has been time for only three in Britain, and the last of them has been completely disrupted by two wars. Professor Dennis Robertson once wrote that we had better wait a few centuries before being sure about their existence (44, p. 295).[1] The coexistence of long and short waves also causes untold difficulties. A very strong boom in one

[1] The figures in parentheses in the text refer to works listed in the Select Bibliography, pp. 56 ff.

of the ten-year cycles, say, may be followed two cycles later by a most vigorous depression and so give the appearance of a longer swing. But no such long cycle exists unless one can demonstrate a clear and regular pattern of mild and severe booms and slumps. In the period we are investigating, the boom to 1873 was unusually pronounced in several different ways; the slump of the early 1890s was very severe too. Are we to see these as the terminal points of a unified period of economic history or as unique events giving only the *appearance* of a long swing? The great home boom from 1897 to 1900 causes confusion too, as careless writers are apt to make comparisons before and after the turn of the century without making clear whether they think this was indeed a turning-point in long-run trends or again just an isolated event. Difficulty can arise out of the choice of indicators. If one uses price data, as Kondratiev, the founder of the long cycle, mainly did, then the series is inevitably dominated by the great price peaks of the last 150 years – 1812, 1873, the First World War – and this immediately poses the question just raised. Were these not just isolated events and not part of a general pattern?

We cannot try to answer such questions in full here, but it is obvious that we must spread our net beyond the confines of the 'Great Depression' years and look at those years in the context of the long-term development of the economy. One final warning: much of our material is inevitably statistical. Except for the price data, the series we employ are by no means completely reliable. Even with prices the construction of an overall index is fraught with problems. The one we use, for instance, represents too heavily movements in foreign trade prices. But these weaknesses may not be too serious if we refrain from jumping to conclusions more sweeping than the figures should rightly allow. We shall have to take care not to take much account of relatively small and short-lived fluctuations and always to look more to changes in our series than to their absolute levels.

Prices

DIAGRAM I on page 12 shows the course of wholesale prices during the nineteenth century. The long-cycle problem is apparent right away. The peaks of 1818 and 1873, the troughs of

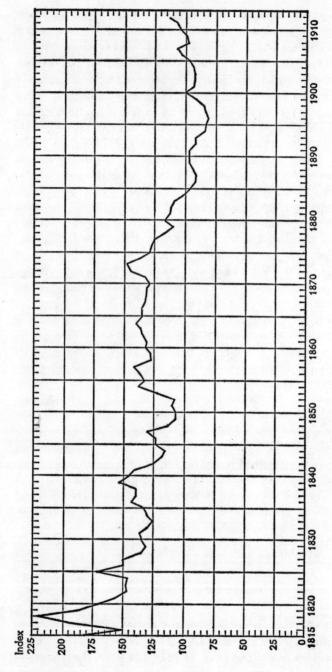

Diagram I. *Wholesale Prices in Britain, 1815–1913 (1900 = 100)*

the late 1840s and the mid-1890s, are clear enough. It is the pattern in between which causes the trouble. We can create almost any trend we like to 1850, depending on the choice of dates; prices may be described as steady on the whole from 1821 to 1841 (treating 1818 as an aberration) or we may say they were falling from 1818 to 1833 and thereafter stable till the late 1840s. After 1852 there were two years of recovery from a deep slump in prices and then a remarkably steady plateau for almost two decades with a jump during the very powerful boom in 1872–3. Hardly a period of *rising* prices as the long-swing analysis postulates. Simply to look at the trough in 1852 and the peak in 1873 is certainly misleading. Even two of the most powerful advocates of the long-cycle analysis once wrote: 'anyone who did not know these waves in advance might conclude that the trend of prices was not falling from 1823 to 1840 or rising during 1853–71'.[1]

But then came the most unmistakable trend of the whole century. For fourteen years, with one slight respite, prices fell without cease, overriding all shorter cyclical fluctuations. There is nothing comparable in the Diagram, even allowing for smoothing out the boom of the early 1870s, and it obviously needs a special explanation. Thereafter the trends were less dramatic – the upswing of a ten-year cycle sent prices up to 1891 with a further fall back to 1896 taking them some 10 per cent below the level of 1887. Then followed a relatively modest recovery to 1914.

It may be that it is right to follow Landes [24] and to treat the years from 1815 to 1897 as a single period of continuously falling prices with a plateau in the middle. One detailed study of price movements has shown that many prices began to fall distinctly during the middle 1860s (36, p. 116). The boom to 1873, it is argued, concealed the real trends which were already under way. Such an analysis lends much support to Landes's point of view. He argues that the cost-reducing effects of a constant stream of innovations were the basic economic elements in the decline. Again this may well be the root cause, but there are some important questions to be asked even so. Why, for example, did such innovations lower prices in the nineteenth but not in the twentieth century? And, despite the long trend, there is something

[1] A. F. Burns and W. C. Mitchell, *Measuring Business Cycles* (1946) p. 440.

special about the plateau and the drastic fall after 1873 which we have to explain. Prices of most other industrial countries follow a similar pattern after 1870, though with differences in detail. As we shall see later, with nearly all of them on the gold standard this was inevitable.

Looking at individual prices in detail we find considerable divergencies. For those which fell most markedly, sugar and petroleum, one can offer special explanations readily enough – the subsidies which were granted for the production of beet sugar on the Continent of Europe, for example, and the transformation in the supply position for oil as new wells were opened up. The smallest falls were to be found among the animal food-stuffs as Table I shows – butter, bacon, mutton, beef, eggs. Indeed the price of eggs rose steadily from 1870 onwards. The explanation here stems from the demand side. As the prices of other food-stuffs fell and as the standard of living began to rise generally, people began to use their higher incomes to vary their diet more and to eat more milk, butter, meat, eggs and fruit. In other words, demand for these foods was income elastic and the price was well maintained. Coffee slumped from 1873 to 1885, rose in the early 1890s above the level of 1870 and began to fall again around 1900.

Table I. *Board of Trade Wholesale Price Indices*
(1871–5 = 100)

	Coal and metals	Textile fibres	Grains	Animal products	Sugar, tea, tobacco, coffee and cocoa	Total index
1871–5	100	100	100	100	100	100
1876–80	66·7	85·4	95·4	102·6	90·2	92
1881–5	60·7	76·9	83·7	98·6	75·1	83·5
1886–90	61·5	66·5	67·7	84·8	56·8	70·6
1891–5	63·6	60·3	66	84·6	53·7	68·3

This appears to have been the result of a distinct cycle of short crops and overproduction covering some fifteen or sixteen years. The price of coal, which dominates the first group in Table I, fell sharply from 32s a ton (London price) in 1873 to 18s in 1878. This was the price of the late 1860s and except for two very unusual boom years, 1900 and 1901, it fluctuated between 16s and 19s until just before the First World War.[1] Apart from the 1870s, therefore, coal prices moved moderately around a straight-line trend. Pig-iron prices were also distorted by the 1873 boom; Scotch pig averaged 54s 6d from 1867 to 1871, reached 117s 3d in 1873 and was back to 56s 5d in 1876–7. It is clearly wrong here to take much account of such famine prices in determining the long-term trends. From the late 1870s until 1899 only in one year (1880) did prices average over 50s and twice – in 1886 and 1888 – slipped a penny below 40s. Here the downward trend is distinct, though it should be noted that the decline came to an end in the late 1880s. This is interesting because it fits in with the view of earlier historians that the 'Great Depression' as any kind of unified period of price movements lasted only until that time. Finally, the price of cotton, which was 5·5d per lb. in 1851–5, reached an average of 27·6d in 1864. It was 8·7d in 1871–5, 6·1d a decade later, 4·2d in 1891–5. Here we face both a return to the pre-Civil War position and general price-reducing effects; distinguishing between them is a difficult task.

We have taken a few examples to show the variations and distortions which may occur. These greatly affect the timing of the price movements in Table I. The first two groups show early falls because of the influence of coal, iron and cotton; grains reflect the collapse of wheat prices during the 1880s; animal products fall less than all others, whereas the fifth column, under the influence of coffee and sugar, has the largest fall. The variations are not difficult to explain, and considering the size of the price-fall it is surprising how many commodities experienced declines close to the average. Thus, although the situation is complex and no single explanation can possibly cover the degree and timing of all sectors, we cannot rule out the possibility of a major overall factor whose influence was modified to varying degrees by other determinants. This is so at least until the late 1880s. As the general price decline thereafter slows down, the random variations of particular commodities become more significant and we cannot be so confident of the effects of general overall factors. We now turn to evaluate some of the explanations of this phenomenon which have been put forward from time to time.

[1] Coal export prices settled at a higher plateau after 1900 (around 12s) than during the 1880s, when they averaged about 9s.

15

Money

THE first explanation is the oldest and is one which could have the all-pervading effects mentioned in the previous paragraph. It arises from a simple form of the quantity theory of money which provides for a direct relationship between the supply of money (and its velocity of circulation), the level of production and the level of prices. 'Long period fluctuations [of prices] are chiefly caused by changes in the amounts of precious metals relative to the business which has to be transacted by them, allowance being made for changes in the extent to which the precious metals are able to delegate their functions to bank notes, cheques, bills of exchange and other substitutes.'[1] The argument was that despite the development of commercial banking, the supply of money in the 1870s and 1880s failed to keep pace with the growth of activity and prices consequently fell. A combination of circumstances slowed down the rate of increase of the world's stock of gold upon which currency supplies were based. For one thing, after 1870 most of the major countries adopted the gold standard. There was a scramble for gold as each sought to build up its reserves so as to be able to maintain a fixed rate of exchange and allow free movement of gold in and out of the country. Sterilisation of gold supplies in this way was accompanied by the absence of any new major discoveries until the end of the 1880s when new mines were opened up in Australia and above all in South Africa, to be followed by the Klondike in 1896.

For many years this view was widely accepted, though none thought of it as by any means the only explanation. During the 1930s opinion changed. A famous article by J. T. Phinney appeared to destroy statistically the link between the gold supply and the growth of bank reserves and currency in Britain (37). There was also the nagging problem of the 'Gibson paradox'. If the fall of prices was caused by the supply of money growing more slowly than production, then this relative shortage should have caused rates of interest to rise. In fact they did the opposite. And

---

[1] Alfred Marshall, quoted in [40] p. 5.

finally there was a reaction among economists against the use of monetary weapons for policy purposes and this feeling seems to have.spilled over into their interpretations of history too.

More recent research enables us to revive the possibility of attributing an important role to money. René Higonnet has demonstrated that the statistics used by Phinney were seriously defective and more careful calculations indicate that the rate of growth of bank money from 1873 to 1895 was considerably lower than in the period of higher prices which followed (19). In twenty-two years, from 1873 to 1895, bank money rose by about 16 per cent whereas during the next nineteen years it rose by 30 per cent. Here we must be careful. The stock of money did indeed grow slowly to 1887 – for the decade after 1877 there was no rise at all – but thereafter it increased quickly. This is in line with the view expressed by Keynes in his *Treatise on Money* that while monetary factors provided an explanation of the price-fall to the late 1880s a different explanation was required for events from 1890 to 1896 when gold was obviously abundant. We have already noted some ambiguity in price movements in these later years and this new point reinforces the suggestion that it is a mistake to view the years 1873–96 as a single period for analytical purposes.

Higonnet's findings for Britain are reinforced by those of Professor Friedman and his followers in the U.S.A. Phillip Cagan, in a detailed study of American experience, found a high correlation before 1914 between price changes and the growth of the money stock.[1] He points out that during what we have identified as the critical years from 1875 to 1887, the rate of growth of the world's monetary stock dropped from the 8 per cent of the 1850s to only 1 per cent. And, as Cagan goes on to argue: 'If one concludes from the evidence that price movements in the United States reflect primarily changes in the monetary stock, the same explanation must hold for all countries, including England, that were on the gold standard and had close commercial ties with the United States. There cannot be one explanation of major long-run price movements for this country and another for England, at least while both countries adhere to the gold standard.'[2] The

[1] P. Cagan, *Determinants and Effects of Changes in the Stock of Money, 1875–1960* (New York 1965). See ch. 3 and also the introduction by Milton Friedman.

[2] Ibid. p. 250.

17

point here is that under the gold standard the price levels of countries trading heavily with each other could not diverge substantially, as rates of exchange were kept stable except within very narrow limits. It has been argued that possibly the relationship between money and prices ran in the opposite direction, money being passive and adapting itself to changes in requirements which were initiated independently. More research is needed here, but Cagan has argued from American data that the major influence does in fact run from money to prices.[1]

There remains the Gibson paradox. Alfred Marshall suggested that what had happened was that the shortage of money had prevented the rate of interest from falling as quickly as it might have done. The growing intercommunication between the world's discount markets made rates more stable, the Bank of England was managing its affairs more efficiently, the absence of wars caused less disturbance in the market; all these factors were tending to pull interest rates down. Professor Ashworth more recently has also seen institutional changes and shifts in the demand for money as possibly keeping rates low (5, p. 174). Attempts at purely theoretical explanations of the paradox are outlined in the note below for those interested.[2] The argument will no doubt continue. Professor Coppock still believes that 'the behaviour of interest rates is the crucial argument against the monetary theory of the price decline' (11, p. 209). This is now an extreme view; the behaviour of money cannot be the sole

[1] Cagan, *Determinants*, ch. 6.

[2] Irving Fisher, followed by Friedman and Cagan, explained the Paradox in terms of the effect of price changes on the market value of bonds whose returns are fixed in money terms. A fall of prices raises the real value of both principal and interest. In so far as borrowers and lenders anticipate these rises in real values, bond prices will tend to be higher and their nominal yields lower. In so far, too, as anticipations of falling prices lag behind the actual fall as they generally seem to do, interest rates will fall with prices in the process of adjusting these rates to the price decline. Or, to put it another way, falling prices increase the *real* interest rate and if this is expected to continue the *market* rate will be depressed because investors will have a greater preference for money and bonds relative to other types of assets, and potential borrowers a reduced preference. See also J. R. Hicks, *A Contribution to the Theory of the Trade Cycle* (Oxford: Clarendon Press, 1950), p. 154, note 1, for an explanation in terms of liquidity preference theory.

explanation of the price fall if only because not all prices moved to the same extent at the same time. It seems, however, that we may have to put money back to where it used to be as a major force in the price movement, particularly if we are prepared to follow Friedman and Petersen in dating the downward trend from the mid-1860s and ending it in the late 1880s.

Professor Rostow's View

IN his book *The British Economy of the Nineteenth Century*, published in 1948, Professor W. W. Rostow constructed an explanation of the long swings in terms of the shifting balance between different types of investment. He distinguished between investment which brings returns quickly in the shape of output of goods – i.e. investment with a short period of gestation – and investment which either is not productive of final goods at all – wars or gold mining – or which brings its returns only after a considerable period of time. Periods of rising prices are characterised by the second type of investment, falling prices by the first. The two decades or so prior to 1870 saw a great deal of unproductive investment in gold mining and wars. In addition, Britain was investing heavily in building railways and other public utilities at home and overseas; that is to say, indulging in investment with a long period of gestation. After 1873, however, prices began to fall partly because the emphasis in investment switched from overseas to home, lowering the period of gestation and bringing quicker returns. There was less unproductive investment and above all the long gestation investment of the earlier decades now began to bear fruit in the form of final products and of lower costs. Investment overseas, gold mining, wars and rearmament characterised the years of rising prices after 1896 once again.

Unquestionably the book represented a tremendous step forward in our thinking about these problems, giving the analysis a dynamic character that it never possessed before. There are difficulties all the same. Rostow has placed his analysis into a pattern of rising and falling price trends which we now feel is no longer tenable. Furthermore, when applied to the years

1873–96 the statistics simply do not bear out his views in detail. The proportion of the national income devoted to overseas investment then was larger, not smaller, than in the preceding period. His definition of unproductive investment is too narrow; he takes little account of house-building which was actively under way in the 1870s and which might be expected to raise most prices except rents. These, in any case, do not appear in our price index. But because a theory turns out to be too ambitious and draws unduly sharp contrasts between home and foreign investment, productive and unproductive investment, periods of rising and of falling prices, we must be careful not to ignore the underlying truths of the argument. The two decades before 1870 did see a succession of major wars which helped to boost the price level – to create the plateau we have identified – in a way that was absent for the following two decades. The Boer War and world rearmament must have had similar effects after the mid-1890s. Quite apart from any monetary effect, the direct demands arising from gold mining were clearly less during the 'Great Depression' years. These demands would be inflationary since no final goods were created to match the incomes made available. It is right, too, to concentrate our minds on the consequences for the world economy of the opening up of new areas and the development of new technologies. Furthermore, if we confine our attention simply to the years from 1873 to 1887, then the proportion of investment going overseas is below normal for the half-century to 1914 and we can accept Rostow's views for that part of the 'Great Depression' far more readily.

Other writers, especially R. C. O. Matthews and Brinley Thomas, have laid stress on the interaction of home and foreign investment in a somewhat different way.[1] We cannot go into detail about this unsynchronised movement of two elements in the economy, but they are certainly extremely important. In the early 1870s their peaks came close together; the subsequent fall in foreign investment in that decade was so steep that only a minor gain in income and no recovery of prices was produced by the rise of home investment to a second peak in 1877. Then again the cyclical peak of activity of 1882–3 was unusual in that neither home nor foreign investment was at a peak. The result was a very

[1] R. C. O. Matthews [29] pp. 215–23 and [30]. B. Thomas, *Migration and Economic Growth* (Cambridge, 1954) ch. 7.

moderate boom which contemporaries found disappointing and which brought only slight price rises. Factors such as these may go some way towards explaining the sagging level of prices and also the low rate of growth of production which we come to later. The difficulty is that we know too little about how and why the two types of investment interacted. It may be accidental; it may be due to complex links between activity, migration, investment and house-construction here and in the United States, as Professor Thomas has argued. We should note, however, that the brief outline above of the interaction of home and foreign investment during the 1870s and 1880s provides a much more gloomy interpretation than that of Rostow. He sees these as decades when the returns are coming thick and fast from current and earlier investment. The interacting process seems to suggest an economy never quite at full throttle.

Reduction in Costs

WE mentioned earlier Professor Landes's view that the whole of nineteenth-century price history can be seen in terms of large and continuous cost-reducing innovations. It is not difficult to point to individual examples of striking reductions in prices resulting from cost-saving innovations. New developments in transport both on land and sea come immediately to mind. The extension and refinement of the Bessemer and Siemens processes for making steel helped to bring the price of rails down from £15 10s in 1873 (or £9 17s 6d in 1874 after the end of the boom) to around £4 in the early 1890s; other technological changes reduced the price of tinplate from 30s in 1874 to under 10s in the mid-1890s, falls which clearly reflected more than the general price decline. But before we get too excited by this approach we must ask one or two questions. First, one we have already mentioned; over the last half-century there have been technological advances of similar magnitude, but on the whole prices have risen. Why, then, did they fall in the nineteenth century? What was different? Were the innovations of greater general importance; or is it that the role of money, the power of labour, the extent of fluctuations have altered? Even if we waive this problem it must be remembered

21

that we are trying to explain a particular price-fall. What was the timing of these cost-reducing innovations? Were they greater in the 1870s and 1880s than in the previous or subsequent decades? Finally, we must never think in terms of supply alone. What was happening to demand? A potentially simple explanation has already become very complicated. Information is sparse and the theory of price that must underlie our analysis quickly becomes fiendishly difficult once the simplifying assumptions have been stripped away.

We can begin with the relatively straightforward question of transport costs. During the eighteenth and early nineteenth centuries the main increases in the productivity of shipping came less from technological changes than from the effects of more extensive markets. This meant that ships spent less time idle in ports and could more often pick up round-trip cargoes. Growing political stability also helped by reducing the need to carry armaments. After 1840, however, there came great technical advances – iron and then steel hulls, ever more efficient engines, machinery for handling rigging and sails. Furthermore there was a marked acceleration in the growth of two-way trade, especially the outward trade in coal from Britain. The opening of the Suez Canal in 1869 was also very important for trade to Australia and the Far East. Professor North's calculations indicate these cost reductions in several ways. Table II shows the movement of freight rates on goods shipped from the U.S.A. to Britain and the Continent.[1] Freight rates were extraordinarily high in 1873 and this distorts the index, but the table shows no downward trend

Table II. *Index of Average Annual U.S. Freight Rates*
(1830 = 100)

1850–4	42·8	(42·2)	1875–9	50·4	(43·3)	1895–9	27·9	(35·9)
1855–9	41·4	(36·7)	1880–4	38·6	(33·4)	1900–4	26·2	(28·3)
1860–4	53·6	(55·1)	1885–9	30·8	(33·5)	1905–9	22·4	(22·0)
1865–9	47·7	(42·2)	1890–4	29·4	(34·5)	1910–14	26·6	(24·2)
1870–4	54·4	(42·5)						

[1] D. C. North, 'The Role of Transportation in the Economic Development of North America', in *Les Grandes Voies Maritimes dans le Monde* (Commission Internationale d'Histoire Maritime, 1965) p. 236.

until the 1880s. Then, however, there is a very sharp fall which continues, though after 1890 at a much-reduced rate, until just before the First World War. The 1880s are the crucial decade, matching then the reductions achieved in the 1830s and 1840s. An index of British tramp-shipping rates falls in a similar way. Taking 1869 as 100, it is still 99 in 1877, then collapses to 59 in 1886, recovers slightly, only to drop to 56 in 1895–6 and to 46 in 1909. The figures in brackets in Table II show the deflated index, or an index of the 'real' price of shipping obtained by eliminating the effects of general price movements from actual freight rates paid. This shows little change from 1850 to the end of the 1870s, a huge fall in the 1880s and further reductions after 1900. For individual commodities we have calculations of the 'freight factor' – the share of shipping freight in the total delivered cost of the goods. Baltic fir timber to London falls from 30·4 per cent in 1863 to 14 per cent in 1884, stops above that level to 1896 and then goes on falling to 1909.[1] Black Sea wheat to Liverpool falls after 1864 (17·9 per cent) to 8·8 per cent in 1886 and begins to fall again after 1896. It is therefore clear that although the fall in shipping rates was an element in the price fall its impact was no more confined within the traditional 'Great Depression' period than other factors we have studied.

Reductions in overland transport rates were important too, though we should remember that where they were built, canals brought much greater reductions in cost over wagons than did railways over canals. The rate on wheat from Chicago to New York fell by 64 per cent for lake and rail and 54 per cent for rail alone over the 'Great Depression' period. We have no space for further illustration but certain general points must be made. Professor North has claimed that his deflated index shows the increase in productivity of shipping – the reduction in the cost of running ships. We must again remember demand as well as supply and some of the fall in real freight rates may have been due to a slackening in the rate of growth of demand for shipping, though to be sure this would be a minor factor. More important, we must take care not to exaggerate the importance of freight rates. We have given examples for bulky commodities, such as wheat and timber, where transport is a major item but it would be far less important for many other goods. Professor Coppock has

[1] Ibid. pp. 239–42.

suggested that at most transport costs would account for only one-sixth of the fall in import prices from 1872–3 to 1895–9 (11, p. 211).

There are also general reductions in costs of production to be considered but here we have less information. Most writers stress the important role of low-cost producers of wheat in the American West in bringing down the price of that commodity, but again we have to ask how far this was due to supply factors, that is to say actual cost reductions, or to changes in demand patterns. Allen Bogue has shown that wheat growers on the Prairie Plains were able to make profits despite the falling prices. This was partly because their transport costs fell more than the price they received for their grain, but he feels that the adoption of new horse technologies was an important cost-reducing factor too. In some industrial processes we have direct evidence of massive cost reductions. Steel we have mentioned. The Solvay process brought the price of soda down from £13 a ton in 1863 to £4 in 1902. The pressure this placed on the makers using the older Leblanc method forced them to reduce their coal consumption, for example, by over a third between 1872 and 1882.

But prices did not necessarily fall at the same time as costs. Take Australian wool. Professor Butlin shows that the 1870s saw both high wool prices and falling unit costs, and with some interruption this went on to 1884. Thereafter prices fell sharply for a decade or more, but now costs were steady if not indeed rising. In the absence of any special demand factors Butlin comments, 'it seems possible that the rate of increase of Australian wool production may have been a major factor in the decline of British wool prices'.[1] It is a cautious statement but we should note that it concentrates on *production*; the fall of costs and the fall of prices did not coincide. The high profits obtained under high prices and falling costs during the 1870s and early 1880s induced a rapid expansion of output which eventually led to lower prices and also because of overstocking of the land and other factors, to rising costs. This 'overshooting process' (Rostow) or 'flooding of the world market', possibly as a result of earlier cost reductions or high prices or both, may well have been important in many directions. It implies narrowing profit margins and, if Bogue is

[1] N. G. Butlin, *Investment in Australian Economic Development* (Cambridge, 1964) p. 175.

24

right, this was not true for wheat producers in part of the American West at least, but it almost certainly applies to British coal owners, for example, facing lower prices after their investment spree during the boom years of the early 1870s.

Demand

IN discussing the relationship between costs and prices we were careful to stress that one must always think of demand too. Why this doubt about the role of costs? Is it conceivable that in a period of rapid growth demand could have been doing anything else but accelerating rapidly? The answer to this second question is that we are not really sure. We do know that the rate of growth of industrial production in Britain slowed after 1870 and of real national income after 1890. We shall discuss this later but it is particularly important because Britain was such a major force in world trade – in 1876–80 she was responsible for 30 per cent of world trade in primary products – and it is changes in the prices of *traded goods* which dominate the trends we are considering. Measurement is difficult because whereas industrial production obviously influences the prices of raw materials, food-stuffs are more likely to be affected by changes in real income. Unfortunately the latter in particular is dependent in considerable measure upon the very price movements we are seeking to explain. However, given the distinct retardation of growth in British industry after 1870 and her relative importance in world trade, it is necessary only to show that there was no marked acceleration of growth in the U.S.A. and Germany to offset this, to make the point, especially as deceleration of French growth for almost two decades after 1882 is well established. Information is unfortunately very sparse prior to 1870 and consequently it is difficult to make comparisons with earlier periods. Frickey's index of U.S. industrial production certainly shows no acceleration during the period and Gallman's figures for real Gross National Product show a distinct retardation.[1]

[1] R. Gallman, 'Gross National Product 1834–1909', in *Output, Employment and Productivity in the U.S. after 1800* (National Bureau of Economic Research, 1966) p. 9.

Table III. *U.S. Gross National Product*
Decennial Rate of Growth at Constant Prices

1839–48 — 1849–58	70%		1884–93 — 1894–1903	36%
1869–78 — 1879–88	65%		1889–98 — 1899–1908	51%
1874–83 — 1884–93	50%		1894–1903 — 1904–1913	49%
1879–88 — 1889–98	36%			

For Germany the figures are much disputed but show no signs of rapid acceleration.

The problem is obviously still unresolved, but there seems in fact to be little evidence of marked upward trends in the other major countries to offset the well-established deceleration of growth of industrial production in Britain. Study of the growth of world output of coal and of iron points in the same direction. The argument will continue, but there is at least a prima facie case for asserting that a deceleration of the growth of world demand was partially responsible for the price fall. To what extent and between what precise dates we cannot yet say. But to return to the first question, why have we bothered with this inconclusive analysis of demand; will not the supply side suffice? The answer to that is really the answer to our whole approach to the price problem. Money, gestation periods, costs, demand; all are tenable answers, all have shortcomings, none is enough on its own. The price-fall was the result of a complex series of circumstances coming together gradually, affecting different products in different ways.

As regards supply we cannot be as confident as we would wish to be that conditions altered greatly from those obtaining in earlier years. We may ask if it is possible to generalise on the basis of the facts established for Australian wool. Unfortunately it is difficult to point to any acceleration in the growth rate of primary products as a whole to account for changes in price levels in accordance with such general 'flooding the market' analyses. But some argue that this is not enough and that we need to study more the difference between actual and potential output of these products – between the amount that *is* produced and the amount that *could be* produced at a given price. Though these may coincide for food-stuffs – as Arthur Lewis wrote, 'food is produced and sold for what it will fetch' – this is not the case with raw materials where actual output adjusts quickly to demand arising from changes in industrial production. Yet price is determined by demand and by potential not actual output, and there is some evidence that potential output of raw materials did in fact accelerate somewhat during the 'Great Depression' years, possibly in part because of the fall in transport costs. Supply factors therefore may have been more significant for raw materials than for food-stuffs. But in the last analysis we need to know considerably more in detail about the reductions in cost of production of particular primary products to bring that part of our analysis on a par with the far more accurate information available on transport costs.

The Recovery of Prices

IF our arguments are to hold good at all, finally we must try to explain the recovery of prices after the mid-1890s. Fortunately our problems here are less serious, provided we do not worry too much about the precise turning-point. This is reasonable because the five years from 1896 to 1900 can be considered as a vigorous cyclical upswing – a home boom topped off by a war. 1895 can be viewed simply as the trough of an eight-year cycle. It is the trend after the turn of the century, a distinctly though not sharply rising one, that we must discuss. The money supply was certainly much augmented by the gold discoveries in Australia, South Africa and the U.S.A. In Britain Higonnet found that bank money rose at almost twice the rate from 1895 to 1914 as in the previous two decades. In addition, there was a renewed burst of Professor Rostow's long gestation investment – gold mining itself, the Boer War, the pre-1914 burst of investment in armaments and new spurts of railway-building. There is evidence of both a recovery of world industrial production and a slowing down in the rate of growth of supply of raw materials and food-stuffs and this despite a continued fall in transport costs. There was a marked fall in American food exports for example, as home demand grew faster than output. Of itself this tells us nothing but the virtual removal from the world market of one major food exporter was probably difficult to replace.[1] As with the price decline, the reversal of the trend was due to a combination of circumstances, interacting to some degree no doubt. But just as the traditional commencement date of the 'Great Depression' has no long-run significance, simply marking the end of a vigorous boom, so its terminal date marks the bottom of a slump not a magical turning-point of a trend.

The Terms of Trade

WHATEVER view we take of the causes of price movements, they in turn affected the economy in several important ways and we look first of all at the relative movements of the prices of imports and exports, or the terms of trade (see Diagram *II*). Though they fluctuated considerably, these movements fitted the traditional turning-points of the 'Great Depression' no better than other series. They tended to move in Britain's favour from the mid-1850s onwards (export prices rose more than import) and soared dramatically during the years of high coal and iron prices from 1871 to 1873. Thereafter they fell back again, so that by the late 1870s they were at the level of a decade earlier. From about 1885 they began to improve slowly but distinctly and, ignoring the Boer War boom, held the gain to 1914. It is more important with the terms of trade than with any other index to have regard to the effect of these high boom years. Professor Kindleberger has shown that fluctuations in the price of coal were a major influence and these together with iron prices were peculiarly volatile in the early 1870s and around 1900 (22, pp. 133–7). If we exclude these years of high export prices and the American Civil War period, our general analysis changes shape considerably. We can stress more the plateau in the terms of trade up to the mid-1880s and the improvement thereafter, whereas historians who do not choose to discount temporary booms think more in terms of an actual worsening of the terms of trade after the Boer War.

[1] In the 1890s, for example, U.S. exports of wheat and flour were between 40 and 50% of the trade of the major exporting countries – U.S., Canada, Russia and Argentina – and her exports of animal food products were 75 to 80% of total exports of these products by the U.S., Argentina, Australia, New Zealand and Russia. See [31] p. 129.

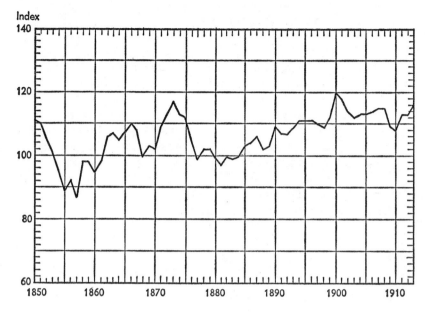

Diagram *II. U.K. Terms of Trade, 1850–1913 (1850 = 100)*
Calculated by dividing an import price index into an export price index. A
rise in the index shows an improvement in the terms of trade for Britain.

Taking the former view, how do we explain the improvement?
To some extent it was the result of this voracious demand for coal
whose price, we have seen, held up while most others were
falling. It was helped too by the sagging price for wheat, another
major element in the terms of trade. If we like the supply
approach we can argue in terms of general productivity movements – that falls in transport and other costs for primary
producers were more marked than those for industrial production.
We would have to exclude British coal production where productivity fell from 1883 onwards, but since Britain was a major
coal exporter this fitted into the pattern nicely. We can argue,
too, that labour was in a better position for reaping some of the
gains of productivity in industrial than in primary producing
countries and thereby influenced relative price movements.
More ominously, it has been suggested that the fact that British
export prices held up reflects a decline in her competitive position.
The statistical analysis is not strong but for what it is worth it
can be shown that the prices of imports into the U.S.A. from

29

countries other than Britain during these years fell substantially in relation to those from Britain (48, p. 10).

We must be careful not to give too much emphasis to this topic because there are so many problems over the actual calculation of the terms of trade. Two points may be made, however. Ignoring the boom periods, the movements were gradual enough to give comfort to those arguing that monetary factors, which would tend to affect most prices in a similar fashion, were important in determining the course of prices. We should bear in mind, too, that the gradual worsening of the terms of trade for primary producers, would tend, in so far as they were not the result of improved productivity, to impair their ability to import manufactured goods. This may possibly have affected the growth of Britain's exports – a point we return to later.

Employment and Wages

WAGES and real wages – wages recalculated in terms of what they will buy – inevitably influenced and were influenced by the course of prices. To the wage earner himself just as important as the level of real wages was the state of employment. There has been much controversy over this last point because it is vital to the question of whether there was a depression in any real sense other than a sag of prices during the years after 1873. Our information is unsatisfactory because at that time no national figures were collected, there being no government unemployment insurance scheme in operation. We have to rely on such trade union figures as are available. Professor Rostow argued that unemployment was no higher on average than in the two preceding or succeeding decades (45, p. 48). Subsequently it has been shown, however, that this conclusion was only reached by juggling with the dates. Unemployment during 1874–95 was clearly higher than during 1851–73 and 1896–1914, the figures being 7·2 per cent compared with 5 per cent and 5·4 per cent respectively. However, we have shown no great affection for these particular dates in this essay so far and there is no need to do so now. Unemployment was indeed remarkably low from 1870 to 1878, with a home boom following the great export spurt to 1873.

30

The high average level of unemployment arose from later events. It was very high in 1879 and for no other recorded period before 1921 did unemployment stay above 7½ per cent for four successive years as it did from 1884 to 1887. In 1888 it was still above 4½ per cent too. There were four more bad years from 1892 to 1895. It has been argued that this phenomenon arose largely out of two factors. First there was a marked fall in the level of house-building, nothing unusual because it had been preceded by a high level of such activity, though this cannot be the whole explanation, for there were very high levels of unemployment in the metal and engineering industries. A second development was a deceleration of effective demand in the face of a constant growth of the occupied population. We discuss the decline in the rate of growth in the next section, but it is worth noticing now that the level of unemployment might have been worse than it was, had there not been a marked fall in the rate of growth of labour productivity. A revival of house-building during the mid-1890s helped to bring

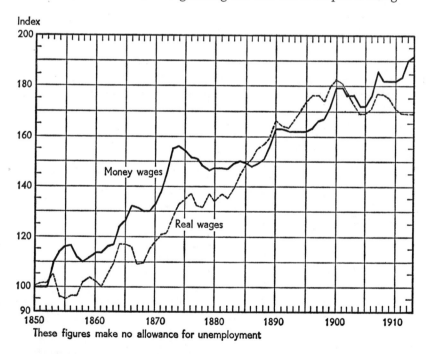

Diagram *III. Money Wages and Real Wages in Britain, 1850–1913 (1850 = 100)*

unemployment heavily down again for six years as it had done two decades before.

All this, however, was not accompanied by any decline in the rate of growth of real wages. These grow at much the same annual rate in the two decades before 1873 as in the two following (see Diagram *III*). This, nevertheless, confuses the real timing, for the 'Great Depression' has no particular meaning for real wages either. Taking 1850 as 100, real wages (making no allowance for unemployment) were still at that level a decade later. By 1865 they had reached 117 and were still at this same level in 1869. Then they surged forward to reach 133 by 1874, the rise of money wages in those years being the fastest known before the First World War. Precisely why this came about we do not know; it may have been partly due to the high prices for iron and coal and the existence of sliding-scale wage agreements in those industries. Possibly even more important is the fact that real wages stayed up so well afterwards. From 1876 to 1888 money wages were very stable, never changing more than plus or minus 2 per cent per annum and with no set trend. With falling prices real wages necessarily eased upwards. A sharp rise in money and in real wages in 1889 and 1890 was followed by six more stable years and then a further rise in money and real wages to 1900.[1]

Why did it happen? Improving terms of trade and income from overseas helped boost the national income and to give a margin for increased consumption over that produced by the now slackening rate of growth of home production. It is clearly not enough to argue, as some writers do, that the rise in real wages was due simply to the fall in prices; it was due also to the ability of wage earners to force wages way up above prices in the boom years and to maintain the money wage plateau in between. Professor Phillips's well-known analysis of the relationship between un-

---

[1] A word of warning is especially important here. The statistics of wages before 1880 are so incomplete that any analysis of their movement must be considered as in large measure speculative. There were certainly important local variations. In Sheffield, for example, real wages rose much less than the national average between 1873 and 1890, possibly because earnings were very high in the 1850s and 1860s, whereas the later years saw Sheffield industries severely hit by the depression. See S. Pollard, 'Wages and Earnings in the Sheffield Trades 1851–1914', *Yorkshire Bulletin of Economic and Social Research*, VI (1954) p. 59.

employment and the rate of change of money wage rates suggests that when the demand for labour is high employers bid up wages, but that workers are reluctant to offer their services at less than the prevailing rates when unemployment is high and so wage rates fall only slowly.[1] In years of rising activity, such as the early 1870s with the demand for labour rising and the percentage of unemployed falling, employers were bidding for labour more vigorously and wages rose more quickly than if the average percentage of unemployment were the same but the demand for labour not increasing. The rate of change of money wages was at its highest when unemployment was decreasing most rapidly. Changes in the cost of living at such times had little or no effect on wages. This is reasonable enough, but what about the remarkable plateau between the early 1870s and the turn of the century? We may need to link an argument on cyclical movements with one related more to long-term trends. Arguing, as some have done in terms of the power of organised labour, it might be suggested that during the highly competitive environment of falling prices, unions were able to squeeze profits between stable wages and market-controlled prices. Even if unions were weak the market kept prices down to the resultant level of costs, and profits would not rise. Certainly the period appears to have seen a marked rise in the share of industrial income going to wages at the expense of profits. The share of wages in the sum of profits plus wages was 52·3 per cent in 1870–4 and 62·2 per cent in 1890–4. But when the trend of prices was reversed in the less competitive environment after 1900 even strong unions could only push up the whole cost and price structure, and prices and profits kept pace with wages. Discounting the rise over the Boer War years, from 1896 to 1914 real wages fell slightly, in very marked contrast to the previous three decades. The role of profit itself is immensely important but we will leave that until we discuss the course of investment and of industrial production.

We must admit frankly that much of this is theoretical and the basic historical work has yet to be done. Half the rise of real earnings for wage earners from 1880 to 1910, for example, was due to people moving into better-paid jobs – not in itself a

[1] A. W. Phillips, 'The Relation between unemployment and the Rate of Change of Money Wage Rates in the U.K., 1861–1957', *Economica*, xxv, 1958.

complete explanation, of course, because we want to know why they were able to do so. The stagnation of real wages after 1900 has been attributed by some in part to the particular difficulties of certain industries, such as the railways, caught between rising costs and prices made inflexible by statute and the coal industry with its steadily falling productivity. Others have seen it as resulting from the contrast between the relatively low level of investment at home and the unduly rapid rise of the adult population during the two decades before the war. From 1891 to 1911 the adult male population under 65 rose by 35½ per cent compared with 24 per cent for the total male population.

Agriculture

NOW we must turn to look at the economy as a whole after 1870, but before tackling our major problem, the decline in industrial growth, we must spend a short time with the agricultural industry, which was once considered the main victim of the 'Great Depression'. It is true that there was a sharp fall in the numbers engaged in agriculture in Great Britain – from 1·6 m. in 1871 to 1·4 m. in 1891 and 1·3 m. in 1901 – but this was nothing new and indeed the largest absolute fall in numbers came in the 1860s. Some sectors of agriculture did suffer seriously from the fall of prices and the industry had to bear all the problems of an extensive structural change taking place over a short space of time with little or no relief from the Government. The difficulties were accentuated, too, by a run of exceptionally bad seasons in the late 1870s. Wheat-producers felt the blasts most savagely. In 1867–76 this crop accounted for 13 per cent of the gross agricultural output of the U.K.: by 1894–1903 it was 4 per cent. In England the fall was from 22 to 7 per cent. Although the prices of oats and barley fell in a similar fashion, most farmers continued to grow these crops to provide fodder and essential straw. Wool prices began to fall in the mid-1860s; a short-lived recovery in 1871–5 was followed by a further collapse until stability was achieved a decade later at some 60 per cent below the level of 1865–74.

In other sectors the difficulties were much less, however. The low prices of grain feeding-stuffs greatly benefited livestock-producers. Rising real incomes increased demand for animal products and less competition was experienced from overseas. True, there were large imports of butter and cheese, but this was offset by the buoyant home market for liquid milk. Imported meat, live or frozen, competed only with low-quality home meat. Between the late 1860s and the mid-1890s the price of best English beef fell by 11 per cent and of mutton and lamb by 8 per cent; imported meat fell by 23 per cent and 30 per cent respectively. They clearly catered for two quite different markets. Prices of meat products in Britain fell less than prices in general and did not commence even that modest decline until the mid-1880s. The shift from arable to livestock was in any case not new; the change to a more mixed pattern of farming had been distinct during the 1850s and 1860s but now moved forward at greater speed. The corn counties of the south and east suffered most of all; the grazing counties of the north and west and those areas most readily serving the requirements of the big towns for milk and vegetables remained prosperous. The contrast between movements of rents, wages and profits in those areas is most marked. Mr Fletcher has shown, for example, that the Earl of Derby's Lancashire rents rose by 18 per cent from 1870–1 to 1896, whereas those for some Cambridgeshire estates fell by 35 per cent (16, p. 421).

The fall in the number of workers on the land was not caused solely by the depression by any means. It was as marked in the north and west as elsewhere and indeed, as we have seen, preceded the fall in prices. The drift arose partly from the pull of competing occupations with higher wages and less exacting hours, partly from a fall in the demand for labour arising out of the introduction of machinery and partly from the switch to less labour-intensive forms of production. The last two were by no means independent factors, though the second was intensified by the sharper fall in prices for arable crops which by and large required the most labour. Productivity in agriculture (measured by value added per worker at constant prices) rose by 15 per cent between 1867–9 and 1886–93 compared with a rise of 23 per cent in industry and mining. Even so, the share of agricultural income (wages and profits) in Net National Income fell from 20 per cent in 1855–9 to 13 per cent in 1870–4 and a little over 6 per cent in

1895–9. Thereafter with a small recovery of agricultural prices and a slackening of rural emigration the share remained fairly stable to the First World War.

Industrial Production

NOW we come to the last and in many ways most important part of our discussion, our analysis of the declining rate of growth of industrial productions in Britain both in total and per head. There is some controversy over the timing of this decline; Phelps Brown dated it from the 1890s, but Coppock demonstrated that it began two decades before and indeed, but for the distortion introduced by the recovery of the cotton industry after the American Civil War, a retardation is apparent from the mid-1860s onwards (see 10 and 38). The statistics for these years are too rough for us to be very precise on that matter, and for the whole period must be treated with caution. They are given in Table IV.[1] Again there is the problem of cyclical distortion arising from the 1873 boom, but the trends, especially of output per head, are too marked to be explained by that factor alone.

Building is excluded because the long cyclical swings distort the

[1] There has been some controversy over the interpretation of the statistics of industrial growth, but an alternative calculation by J. F. Wright from the same index as that used by Coppock and again excluding building shows unmistakably the declining rate of growth, though it does not closely pinpoint the timing of the change.

Industrial production	Percentage growth per annum %
1800–09 — 1830–39	3·1
1810–19 — 1840–49	3·5
1820–29 — 1850–59	3·5
1830–39 — 1860–69	3·0
1840–49 — 1870–79	2·9
1850–59 — 1880–89	2·4
1860–69 — 1890–99	2·1

See J. F. Wright, 'British Economic Growth 1688–1959', *Economic History Review*, 2nd ser., XVIII (1965) p. 407.

Table IV. *Average Annual Real Growth Rates of British*
Industrial Production (*excluding building*)*

	Total		Per head	
1847–53 — 1854–60	3·5	(3·0)	2·4	(2·1)
1854–60 — 1861–65	1·7	(3·5)	0·6	(2·3)
1861–65 — 1866–74	3·6	(2·8)	2·4	(1·3)
1866–74 — 1875–83	2·1	(2·1)	0·9	(0·6)
1875–83 — 1884–89	1·6	(1·6)	0·2	(0·0)
1884–89 — 1890–99	1·8	(2·0)	0·4	(0·4)
1890–99 — 1900–07	1·8	(2·0)	0·2	(0·3)
1900–07 — 1908–13	1·5	(1·5)	−0·2	(−0·3)

* Figures in brackets are for industrial production, excluding the cotton industry as well as building.

pattern of industrial growth. It was a major form of activity and we were careful to bring it into our discussion of employment and later we shall mention it in connection with capital formation, but the figures for industrial activity alone will reflect the impact that building had upon that sector of the economy. The second column is the more significant for our present purposes because differences in the rate of growth and composition of population can seriously affect total production. This is particularly true of the U.S.A. where total growth was much more spectacular than *per capita* growth.

The differences between Phelps Brown and Coppock arise largely because the former is measuring home-produced *income per head* whose rate of growth did not begin to slacken until just before 1900, whereas the latter is looking at *industrial production*. The gap between these two is a puzzling one.[1] Partly it is closed by a known downward bias in the production index, and Mr Feinstein has suggested that it arose partly from the fact that non-industrial incomes (services, trade, professions) grew at a much more rapid rate than industrial incomes. Unfortunately

[1] This gap cannot be closed, as has been suggested, by including income from abroad and improving terms of trade because Phelps Brown's calculation tries to exclude these factors. Mr Feinstein's correction of these calculations [15] still shows home-produced real income per head rising from £67 in 1870–4 to £86 in 1895–9 and then falling to £85 in 1910–14. (These figures at constant 1890–9 prices.)

we know little about this sector of the economy – sometimes known as the tertiary sector – but it is important to remember that in high-income countries, and above all in a centre of world trade and finance such as Britain, it was to gain growing significance. Total consumption per head was influenced significantly by external factors, the improving terms of trade and the rising trends in other sources of overseas income. Consequently real national income per head rose considerably more than our other indicators. This is an important point, for it is reasonable to argue that consumption is the final aim of all economic activity.[1] However, we shall concentrate on industrial production partly because we know so much more about it, but most of all because its trends were of the greatest significance for the long-run development of all sectors of the economy, including the standard of living. Consumption and production cannot, of course, logically be separated because the two-way flow between them is so important. We might argue, for example, that the fall in real wages after the turn of the century helped to slow down the rise in productivity by constricting the market opportunities. But then we must ask why the sharp rise in real wages before that date did not have the opposite effect? Perhaps it did, and was offset by other less favourable influences: perhaps most of this rise in real consumption was taken up through rising imports. We simply do not know.

Finally we should note that a now familiar problem faces us again here: how do we treat cycles of unusual amplitude? The high level of production and productivity around 1900 makes two views possible. One can write of growth up to this peak and stagnation afterwards to 1914, or one can argue that the rise of 1897–1900 was a flash in the pan and ignore it in looking at the long-term trends. In line with our former arguments we shall take the second approach, but the reader should remember the other point of view.

Some comparative indicators for other countries are shown in Table V. These figures differ from those in Table IV in representing manufacture per head of total population, not occupied population. In that respect they are most unsatisfactory and are intended simply to indicate orders of magnitude. Now it has been argued very forcibly that what we have here is a statistical illusion. It is easy, so it is said, to achieve high percentage rates of

[1] See Addendum, p. 62.

Table V. *Percentage Annual Increase in Manufacture*
per Head of Population

	U.K.	Germany	U.S.A.
1871–75 — 1881–85	0·6	1·7	2·7
1881–85 — 1896–1900	0·9	3·9	2·1
1896–1900 — 1911–13	0·7	2·5	3·2

growth where the starting-point is low. Producing twenty steam engines instead of ten gives a 100 per cent rate of growth but if you are turning out 1000 you need another 1000 to reach this same rate. As the starting-point rises it becomes progressively more difficult to maintain the same growth rate. The arithmetic is obvious enough and if one is making extreme contrasts in narrow sectors of an economy as in the example given, the point possibly has some validity. For whole economies and with the less extreme comparisons concerning us here the argument does not hold. In the first place, though the absolute amount required to obtain any percentage increase is lower, the economic base from which the rise is derived is that much lower too; conceptually there is no difference in the capital/output ratio, though it may well be higher with low absolute levels of output because of indivisibilities of capital equipment. In the second place the argument is belied by historical experience, especially since 1945 when remarkably high growth rates have resulted from technological change. But Patel has shown that for the two decades before 1914 France, Germany, the U.S.A. and Italy all enjoyed rising rates of industrial growth.[1] In any case, even accepting the illusion, there was no discrepancy in absolute size of output large enough to account for the differences shown in Table V. U.S. industrial output in 1881–5 was equal to that of Britain and that of Germany little below in 1914. It is worth noting too that the rates of growth for these countries were higher than those achieved by Britain at *any* time. A late start to industrialisation may bring advantages of a *real* kind, but we shall come to that later.

Professor Ashworth has examined the possibility that changes in working conditions may have lowered productivity in Britain (7, p. 31). He considers the effects of illness, hours of work,

[1] S. J. Patel, 'Rates of Industrial Growth in the Last Century, 1860–1958', *Economic Development and Cultural Change*, IX (1961).

holidays, variations in the numbers of non-productive people, such as paupers and prisoners, and changes in the extent of casual employment, but concludes that these probably made for improvement rather than the reverse. He points to technical weaknesses in the index of production and to its failure to make allowance for quality changes, but again feels that these account for no more than a small amount of the changes in growth rates. Structural changes in employment saw a relative contraction in the textile and clothing industries with low productivity while the gainers were metals, engineering, mining and public utilities, all with much higher levels of productivity. The same resulted from the transfer of labour from agriculture, indeed, after 1870, from that sector of farming with lower than average output per man. These shifts must have tended to raise productivity to 1900 at least. After 1900 we know that less labour was being made available from agriculture, productivity in cotton was stagnant and was falling fast in coal mining. This last would not tend to lower the index, however, because the absolute level of productivity in this rapidly growing industry was well above the average. We have some clues here in explaining the low levels of growth in those last years, but we are further away than ever from understanding the long-term decline.

Can our explanation lie in a low level of capital formation? Kuznets's figures, given in Table VI, show that net domestic capital formation was relatively low in Britain.[1] Why should this have been so? It has been suggested that overseas investment deprived the home market of funds. This was certainly the case for some forms of investment such as house-building and that undertaken by railways and local authorities, but as regards industry the evidence is less clear. Some have argued that money for overseas and home industrial investment came from quite different sources and they only marginally competed against each other. An alternative argument is that the capital market was poorly geared towards the supply of funds for industry at home. There is probably some force in this point but there were so many sources of finance, many of an *ad hoc* nature, and our knowledge so limited that it is impossible to know just now what weight to give to it. The problem is to assess how far industrial growth was inhibited by institutional difficulties of this kind and how far it

[1] S. Kuznets, 'Long-term Trends in Capital Formation Proportions', *Economic Development and Cultural Change*, IX (1961) 10.

Table VI. *Net Domestic Capital Formation as a Percentage of Net Domestic Product*

U.K.		Germany		U.S.A.	
1855–74	7·0	1851–70	8·5	1869–80	13·9
1875–94	6·8	1871–90	11·4	1889–1913	12·9
1895–1914	7·7	1891–1913	15·0		

is accurate to argue that money did not flow into business because industrialists did not wish to borrow. The small size of many companies and the traditions of self-finance were serious hindrances. British industry was noticeably less involved in the merger movements of the last quarter of the nineteenth century than either her American or German counterparts. In so far as a major motive of these amalgamations was the creation of effective marketing and distributive organisations, it is well to recall that it is precisely in this area of business activity that British industry came in for most criticism. That the banking system failed to provide the guidance and drive towards investment, technological change and amalgamation that was found in Germany is indisputable, but this is a different matter from a deficiency in the supply of funds.

Whatever the answer to these questions, one major source of finance for industry was industrial profits and variations in their level were of high importance in determining the trends in industrial investment. Evidence for the years after 1870 suggests that such investment varied more than proportionately with changes in profits. When profits fell, for instance, industrial investment declined to a greater extent. Probably at those times entrepreneurs used such profits as they made to buy foreign securities or to maintain dividends. Now, as we have already seen, a major feature of the British economy after 1876 was the low level of such profits. True, they rose during the late 1890s, but the recovery lasted for only seven years – the last two of these seeing no actual gain – compared with the nineteen years of low profits which preceded it and the ten years of similar conditions which were to follow. This revival of domestic investment after 1895 was clearly not the reversal of a trend, as concentration on the 'Great Depression' might suggest, but a temporary cyclical boom stimulated by a number of specific factors.[1] Among these we may include the low rate of interest, the naval building programme, the switch of rentiers from foreign investment into home house-building, the cycle and electricity boom, as well as the effects of the previous long lay-off from investment. How, then, can we explain the long stagnation in profits and industrial investment? We shall try to answer this from two points of view. We shall see if there were objective factors hindering industrialists – the timing of investment opportunities, the nature of the market situation for example. And we shall ask if there were any powerful reasons why, given a tendency towards lower profits, British industrialists were unable to fight back, re-equip and develop new products in place of the less profitable old ones.

We must be careful not to be concerned exclusively with the absolute level of investment, for recent research has cast some doubt on the importance of capital accumulation *per se* compared with changes in techniques and in the organisation of business. Even so, statistics covering many countries over the last century seem to demonstrate a correlation between growth rates and the investment income ratio. The real problem is deciding the causal sequence. Does higher growth result in higher investment or does higher investment cause growth? Capital utilisation is certainly important too. Professor Ashworth has questioned whether with more and more elaborate plant being installed and

[1] Feinstein's calculations [15], both of the share of profits in industrial income (profits and wages) and in national income, show their relative decline after the mid 1870s and the purely temporary rise two decades later very clearly.

	Profits/Industrial income %	Profits/National income %
1860–64	45	24·2
1865–69	46	26·4
1870–74	47·7	29·4
1875–79	43·3	26·1
1880–84	42·6	25·7
1885–89	42·2	25·2
1890–94	37·8	22·7
1895–99	40·6	24·9
1900–04	39·0	23·7
1905–09	39·5	23·5
1910–14	39·2	23·2

given the shorter working day and limited use of shift work, anything like the optimum use of this equipment was obtained. 'There must be doubt whether processes using new machinery were operated for as much of the available time as they had been earlier when they were much less mechanised.' (7, p. 19.) These conditions may have resulted in a lower rate of return and discouraged further investment. Slow growth can certainly become cumulative because it diminishes the incentive to install new capacity, offers more limited opportunity to try out new methods and makes workers more resistant to change. Ashworth points, too, at new forms of investment which brought low rates of return in the short run anyway – to the development of dormitory suburbs and the pressure this put on public services with consequent under-utilisation because of the need to build up to peak demand. There was investment in holiday resorts, social investment in remote railways, a rise in education expenditure and, worse still, the creation of an educational bias which favoured the production of clerks and shopkeepers over skilled workers. There is much in all this; much against it as well. The railways of the north of Scotland, for example, were the most profitable in Scotland to 1914 and there was much wasteful duplication in earlier periods too. Such peripheral investment was in any case very small. It is not clear that the trend of house-building was higher than in earlier periods and in any case production did not rise faster in industry when house-building was depressed. Even more tellingly, the share of Gross Domestic Capital Formation in Britain devoted to all construction was around 45 per cent from 1855 to 1914 compared with 65 per cent in Germany and 60 per cent in the U.S.A.[1] The figures are crude, but the contrast is striking and a considerably higher share of our admittedly low investment went into producers' equipment.

But to get back to our search for the inability of British industry to break through its difficulties. Some see the problem as an accident of timing. The rate of growth of earlier years, they argue, had been sustained by a series of major innovations, but by the

[1] S. Kuznets, op. cit. p. 38. Statistics for the capital/output ratio – the relationship between the size of the capital stock and the level of annual output (or figures for increases in these two) are very unreliable. Certainly they do not show variations over the period in question which are too large to be outside the margin of statistical error, so that we are unable to extend our analysis far in that direction.

1890s the rate of extension of steam power and of steel had markedly declined. Increasing returns from fuller utilisation of our railway system and from the general transition from the domestic to the factory system had largely ended by that time too. Mr Musson cogently supports this view along the lines first propounded by Professor Schumpeter that growth come in leaps and bounds as a result of discontinuities in major technological innovations. A sophistication of the argument to cope with differential rates of growth sees Britain's competitors growing fast through the incorporation of these new methods at a time when the British economy had almost literally run out of steam. The difficulty is that in a technological sense it hadn't. Mr Musson has been quick to point out that the spread of steam power and the replacement of iron by steel was at its height during the 1870s and 1880s, precisely those decades when Britain's growth began to slacken. After that time the absence of new, all-pervasive innovations may have contributed to a low rate of growth, though it is hard to understand why Britain's competitors did not suffer in the same way. We are, therefore, no further forward at all in understanding the crucial weakness of British industry in taking up new industries, and remain quite in the dark over the retardation of growth of the earlier decades.

Many have suggested that Britain suffered a positive disadvantage from her early start in industrialisation. Theoretically this line of thought is all wrong. The early starter has the greater resources to undertake new investment. The fact that old plant and old locations are actually in existence should be no handicap; capital invested is capital sunk, bygones are bygones and if it pays a newcomer to buy certain plant it pays the older producer to scrap whatever he has and buy the new too. The latecomer may learn from his predecessors, avoid mistakes, take short cuts – abstain from building canals and go straight for railways, for example. This, rather than any statistical illusion, may give him a higher rate of growth but it offers no reason why the newcomer should *overtake* the early starter technologically.[1]

In practice there is more to it. The early starter may find it hard, for institutional or psychological reasons, to break away

[1] The coal industry provides a good example of the process whereby Britain had gained a great lead, but by 1914 found others catching up. Largely for the unavoidable reason of having to utilise poorer seams to

from old methods and locations; the skills and practices of both management and trade unions may be unsuited to the new industrial environment but be deeply resistant to change. The chemical industry's unwillingness to abandon the old Leblanc method of making soda in favour of the Solvay process introduced on the Continent in the 1870s is a case in point. One newcomer – Brunner Mond – did take it up effectively, but most of the other makers fell back upon a defensive alliance and kept to the old ways. One problem was that the profitability of the old method fell only slowly, for the sale of by-products held up the process of decline. The bottom did not fall out of the market, as it did with aluminium for example, and make a complete readjustment imperative.

There is, too, the idea of related costs. The point here is that individual industrial processes are closely interlinked with each other, and frequently advance in one sector may not be made without corresponding changes in other dependent stages. A well-known example is the difficulty of changing the size of wagons on the railways. Terminal facilities, tracks, tunnels were geared to the smaller size and would all have to be changed to accommodate the larger type. Investment in wagons would require extensive investment throughout the whole system. Thus it is argued that the latecomer is spared these interconnecting problems; he can build his track to suit the new wagons from the first. Where large-scale investment is involved, as with railways, the argument is persuasive; with smaller-scale operations it is hard to understand why new firms should not arise in the early-starting country to take up cost advantages just as easily as in the new.

Difficulties such as these have been described as being the result of over-commitment to the older industries, with the suggestion that this may be regarded as the reverse of the idea that German industry gained momentum because of its 'irresistible urge' to invest in the newer industries (43). We might wonder

---

obtain such a large output her productivity was falling sharply but still remained the highest in Europe. The British output per man in coal obtained in the early 1880s was never approached by any other European nation to 1914. It was then 20% above the German level. By 1914 they were about equal, though British productivity was still 30% above that in France and Austria and 60% above that in Belgium and Russia.

if naming in this way takes us any further in understanding the origins of the urges to go into new or stay in older industries. It is important to remember, however, that Britain retained a wide lead in many industrial sectors to 1914. Most of these had their roots in the industrial revolution; cotton textiles and textile machinery, heavy machine tools, custom-built locomotives, ships and steam engines. Some of them were to go into decline after the war but continued investment in them before 1914 was justified by their relative profitability. Some say that, by so investing, British industrialists were maximising short- not long-run interests, but without an improper use of hindsight it is hard to see any meaning in this. What reason could there be for not investing in cotton mills in 1905 when profits expected and realised up to the war were comparable with any elsewhere? And if Britain was wrong to go on making steel rails because future demand was to be poor, were the countries of South America to go without? Were the world's steel-makers to say 'we will not make them for you; our crystal balls tell us that in twenty years demand will have collapsed'? Was it unwise to reap the advantage of favourable prices and satisfy the avid demand for coal from Europe even though the future problems this raised were acute indeed? Britain was surely right to develop these industries as she did and in fact one of her big problems arose from not keeping up with her competitors in one of them – steel-making. It was unfortunate that this inheritance from the past should lead to so many blind alleys. That, however, was a difficulty of the future not a contributor to falling rates of growth before 1914. More serious was the fact that the traditions created by these industries were not always conducive to the development of new industries side by side with the old. The lack of interest and of the necessary skill on the part of steam-engine makers in building diesel engines was one example. The inability of engineers raised in craft traditions to undertake the wholesale rethinking of productive processes necessary to manufacture by mass-production methods was another.

Analyses in terms of these complex links with the past are more convincing than arguments based on the particular faults of British business men. Certainly it is true that public opinion and the social structure were less favourable to the recruitment of entrepreneurs than in some countries overseas. Social mobility was impeded by the class system and moreover there were

46

important sources of power and prestige besides business. Birth, family, education, behaviour, manners, accent played a dominant role in determining social standing, whereas elsewhere more emphasis was placed on a man's success in his job as measured by the income he achieved. The argument is convincing when contrasting British and American industrial achievements but less persuasive in comparison with Germany, for it is hard to believe that this kind of class consciousness was less powerful on the Continent than it was here in Britain. The problem is that entrepreneurial behaviour was only partly dependent upon the social forces within any society; it was also very powerfully influenced by purely objective economic forces. It has been argued that British entrepreneurs were apathetic towards their businesses. As second- and third-generation owners, enthusiasm and application for their work, we are told, were steadily diminishing. It is hard to evaluate such vague arguments.[1] It is as futile to pick out a few successful names and to argue that these were representative of the whole as to suggest that all business men suffered from 'third-generation decline'. Most firms in our period were nowhere near the third generation and of those that were, one can find as many favourable examples as unfavourable. There were wide sectors of British industry – of engineering in particular – consisting of tiny establishments run by ignorant and small-minded men, but these were present in all countries and we need to know that they were worse or more common in Britain. In particular we must beware of comparing their behaviour with that of the modern giants in competing countries.

Our only detailed study, that of the steel industry, has, to be sure, pointed to weaknesses arising from family control (14). How typical this was we do not know, but some of the problems revealed in that book were of a different and more fundamental order. Entrepreneurs and managers in Britain were deficient in technical and scientific knowledge; foremen and operatives were equally poorly equipped. The whole system of education – not

[1] The most amusing version of this entrepreneurial-decline argument came from the Master of a Cambridge college who attributed much of Britain's deficiencies to the invention of false teeth! He argued that this enabled older industrialists to eat better and live longer and also be less embarrassed at attending Board Meetings, thus continuing for longer than before their conservative influence on industrial behaviour.

just technical education – was inadequate compared with those in Germany and the U.S.A. Consequently the preference for the practical over the theoretically-trained man, itself a legacy of an early start in industrialisation, persisted into an age when industries old and new were becoming more science-based and 'rule of thumb', and 'a nose for money' were not enough. There were brilliant exceptions – among the steam engineers and the newer machine-tool makers for example – but the evidence of an overall weakness in this regard is strong. Yet we must try to be judicious even over this. The lack of interest in systematic research has been seen as the basic reason for the British deficiency in some branches of the chemical industry (1, ch. 9). Yet Professor Barker has shown that in the manufacture of glass the secret of success was not to do your own research and development, which usually resulted in losses, but to have a good intelligence service and to pay royalties for a successful process (1, ch. 10). The chemical industry's failure was probably more one of a lack of general alertness towards new developments than of originality.

In a similar way it has been argued – more powerfully perhaps at the time than it is now – that the opposition of workers and their unions hindered the adoption of new industrial methods. It would be idle to deny that the point has some validity; the great lock-out of engineering workers of 1897 arose out of difficulties over the manning of new types of machinery. But to think of this kind of restriction in isolation is to misunderstand the fundamental problem – the striking lack of understanding between management and men. As one foreign observer noted at the time:

> Nothing is more frequent than the remark that the workingman does not need more than so many shillings a week. . . . This view among employers has prevailed for so long and is so nearly universal that their every effort is to obtain more work for a traditional wage rather than to decrease the cost of production by means which will justify a higher wage. . . . Workingmen have come to accept the view widely too and it is the acceptance of this theory of status which is at the bottom of the deadlock in British industry.[1]

[1] Eleventh Special Report of the Commissioners of Labour, *Regulation and Restriction of Output* (Washington, 1904) p. 752.

48

This mutual hostility was not universal – several major engineering firms ignored the 1897 struggle, for example, as they had already arrived at satisfactory manning agreements with their workers – but it was certainly widespread and was hardly conducive to the acceptance of more modern techniques of production and control by either party.

One may therefore distinguish many ways in which Britain's past contributed to her current weaknesses between 1870 and 1914 but we are faced with a nagging feeling that none of these arguments is absolute. Why did she not break with the past to a greater degree despite the handicaps? An important point here arises out of the state of market demand, which it is suggested, acted as a serious depressant to growth. This was true of exports above all, for their rate of growth dropped off markedly. By volume exports of manufactured goods rose 4·8 per cent per annum from 1854 to 1872 and 2·1 per cent per annum from 1876 to 1910. Some of the explanation may be a deceleration of world trade in manufactures as a whole but in the latter period this was still rising at 2·55 per cent per annum. The rise of new competitors and the growth of tariffs were important independent factors at work. Not only this, but, with important geographical advantages on her side, Germany was able to establish huge market advantages in western and eastern Europe as the United States did in Canada. It was precisely in these areas that the demand for the products of the newer industries – electrical goods above all – was so high. Temin has shown that in steel-making, even if Britain had been able to bring her costs below those of Germany, the industry's rate of growth from 1890 to 1914 would have risen only from 3·4 to 4·6 per cent per annum and the German fallen from 9·6 to 9 per cent, so great was the German advantage in the market as a result of tariff policies and also, in this instance, in resource costs.[1] The slower rate of growth itself then produced a technological lag large enough to account for differences in costs without need to bother with entrepreneurial weaknesses, significant though these may have been. It is true that the weakness in Britain's exports was probably as much a consequence as a cause of slow growth but there are clear

[1] P. Temin, 'The Relative Decline of the British Steel Industry 1880–1913', in H. Rosovsky (ed.), *Industrialization in Two Systems* (New York, 1966) p. 149.

exogenous factors at work. Unfortunately the existence of relatively easy and in some ways protected markets in Empire countries induced among business men a tendency to shift in that direction rather than to cut costs or find new products to hold markets in Europe and North America.

At home peculiar market factors inhibited certain strategic industries. Electrical engineers found cotton and mining slow to electrify for perfectly good reasons in each case; in engineering and shipbuilding, where the economics were right, electrification went forward rapidly. The low price and wide use of gas inhibited the use of electricity for lighting; the extensive rail network inhibited its use for traction. Makers of locomotives, bridges, agricultural machinery, firearms and machine tools all had their own market problems (see 49). Certainly a market is not an objective fact, but is partly created by the seller and one may reasonably ask why British manufacturers were not more vigorous in seeking to overcome their difficulties. They were generally regarded as poor salesmen at the time and there is no reason to doubt the validity of this criticism, though one must always beware of writers who on one page argue that the British failed to reap the benefits of standardisation and on the next state that they failed to pay sufficient regard to the individual needs of their customers.

An entirely different line of argument is to explain the greater productivity of labour in the United States in terms of factor costs (see 18, especially chs V and VI). The price of labour there was relatively higher than in Britain compared with the differences in the price of capital in the two countries. Consequently American entrepreneurs substituted capital for labour, used more mechanised processes and raised the productivity of labour so as to be able to meet the high supply price they had to pay to draw it away from frontier agriculture. Much research needs to be carried on into these problems; it is suggested, for example, that it was not so much that the Americans used more capital within a given technological framework but that they were more able to develop entirely new technologies, many of which offered great advantages whatever the relative prices of capital and labour, and which were only slowly adopted in Britain for some of the reasons just discussed. Whatever the reasons, once the pattern of capital intensive methods was established in the U.S.A. it continued to be used even though the original force behind it had disappeared. This characteristic type of investment activity achieved a momentum of its own which new supplies of cheap immigrant labour did not modify, but made it more profitable to exploit. With lower labour costs the above line of argument cannot be applied to Germany but still it is argued that for whatever reason, German industry developed a desire for technological progress which became an irresistible urge to her entrepreneurs. It is a perfectly valid approach so long as one knows the origins of the pattern which has been set. With the U.S.A. we have a tentative theoretical analysis; with Germany we have to rely on less precise arguments, which of course also apply in some measure to the U.S., based on technological education, the role of the banks, the market and the early start.

It is apparent that there is no single explanation of Britain's relative decline. We can only bring out the main factors and seek to eliminate those based on poor reasoning or inadequate research. The statistics probably underestimate Britain's rate of growth, but this only closes the gap to a minor degree. We have to explain why investment was so inadequately carried out and capital equipment so poorly utilised. There may have been institutional problems but the heritage of Britain's early start and the peculiar market difficulties of the late nineteenth century are among the most positive reasons we can propose. To use the concluding sentence of Professor Habakkuk's book: 'Such lags as there were in the adoption of new methods in British industry can be adequately explained by economic circumstances, by the complexity of her industrial structure and the slow growth of her output and ultimately by her early and long sustained start as an industrial power.' (18, p. 220.) It may be that after all is said and done, the entrepreneur and his shortcomings remain to provide the residual explanation for Britain's weaknesses but such a view is hardly helpful because it tells us nothing about the relative importance of this residual element. The patchiness of Britain's experience of business behaviour and the undoubted fact that in important sectors of industry she was fast making good her technological deficiencies in the decade before 1914, may suggest that we should treat this part of the explanation with a good deal of reserve. This is important because it would be misleading to stress only the relative decline of British industry in aggregate. Though it had not gone far enough greatly to influence the productivity figures, the industrial structure and its skills were in process of far-reaching readjustment by 1914. The war was to create a need for much faster change but it would be totally wrong to leave the impression that the pre-war era was one of complete industrial stagnation.

We can emphasise this same point in a rather different way. We have been discussing what economists call a macroeconomic question, one related to the economy as a whole, the total output of its industry. It is vital that we should do so because here is one of the prime determinants of our standard of living and of our position in the world. We have looked, too, at certain macro-economic explanations – the level of total investment, of total industrial profits, of total exports. Again, these are vitally important because they show the overall trends in the economy. But we can never fully answer our questions at this level. We must get down to the particular industry and to particular firms in these industries. Almost invariably we find firms comparable in efficiency with the best overseas. But we need to ask how representative are the best, what is the gap between them and the average, and how does this compare with the distribution in overseas countries? It has not been possible to show this here largely because our knowledge of these matters is so thin. The general points on entrepreneurship, education, research, profitability, and so forth, are all highly relevant, but in the end we shall have to look at them again in this more detailed context.[1]

The final word here should be one of warning. The statistics we have used are not precise; they are not accurate enough for us to be certain about absolute levels at all. Where, however, they show a distinct trend over time they are accurate enough for us to feel that here is something that needs an explanation. We should not be too worried by the negative movement of productivity after 1900, for example, because the inaccuracy of the figures and the distorting effects of the boom of the turn of the century are all complicating issues. It is enough to know that the rate of growth of productivity had been falling steadily for thirty or more years and that this was in marked contrast to Britain's main competitors. This is all we have tried to explain.

[1] See M. M. Postan, 'A Plague of Economists', *Encounter*, Jan 1968, and for an attempt to analyse one industry from this point of view S. B. Saul, 'The Machine Tool Industry in Britain to 1914', *Business History*, x (1968).

Conclusion

IT must be obvious to any reader of this book that there is a long way to go before we come near to a full understanding of the basic forces affecting the British economy at the end of the nineteenth century. It is directly apparent, though, that even when much more research has been carried out, no uni-causal explanation for any of the phenomena discussed here, will be arrived at. We can only hope to become more sure of the relative importance of various factors and to strive for greater statistical and analytical precision wherever possible.

To try to bring some clarity to a confused pattern of events we have broken up the problems into constituent parts, outlining the explanations proffered for each. At this final stage it is important to stress again the interconnections which have emerged. In particular we should remember that the movement of prices and the retardation of growth were closely linked. The swings of home and foreign investment are said to have brought both low growth and sagging prices in the late 1870s and 1880s and again from 1901 to 1910. Lower prices squeezed profits to the benefit of wages and probably this led to lower industrial investment. This is a crucial relationship because falling prices did not necessarily lead to a prolonged reduction of investment in other industrialising countries. The effect upon investment of changes in consumption at home is unfortunately a completely open question. Indeed we know far too little about the forces affecting the supply and remuneration of labour. The relative changes in international trade prices moved against Britain's suppliers and by so doing helped to raise the standard of living at home, but the reduced purchasing power it entailed overseas may have been an important factor in the retardation of British exports and, through them, of growth. Why British business men did not react more vigorously we have tried to explain, but we should always remember one point not made in the body of this study. The events of the 1870s and 1880s, whatever the factors underlying them, caused a serious decline in business confidence. The unusual economic environment may well have lowered expectations and in this way reduced the level of industrial investment. It is an intangible influence, but contemporary accounts suggest it was not an insignificant one.

As regards the 'Great Depression' itself, surely the major outcome of modern research has been to destroy once and for all the idea of the existence of such a period in any unified sense. The last quarter or so of the nineteenth century was a watershed for Britain as competition developed overseas and the rate of growth markedly slackened. But the process was probably under way before 1870 and most certainly continued unabated – at least in statistical terms – after 1900. The terms of trade changed their movement in the middle of the period and continued in the new direction well after 1895. Low profits ruled to 1895 *and* after 1901. The great boost to real wages came in the boom to 1873 and the process was repeated again from 1896 to 1900. Real freight rates did not begin to fall until about 1880 and continued to do so almost to 1914. The downward trend in prices – traditionally the dominant feature of the 'Great Depression' – may also have been under way by the mid-1860s and in several respects had ended its movement by the mid-1880s.

This is not to ignore the fact that at some time during the last quarter of the nineteenth century Britain and several countries overseas went through unusual and worrying economic experiences which sometimes they characterised at the time as 'a great depression'. What is in question is the suggestion that this was a special feature of the years 1873–96. German and American industry suffered a prolonged depression in the 1870s, for example, but most certainly not in the following decade. The French economy, on the other hand, relapsed into stagnation from 1881 to the mid-1890s. Undoubtedly the fall of prices and the impact this had upon agriculture in particular in many parts of the world contributed to the feeling of gloom. Undoubtedly, too, it was a period of rapid change and disturbance. All this, however, is very different from picking out the years 1873–96 as having a peculiar significance either nationally or internationally except, possibly, in so far as prices are concerned, and even this as we have seen is much open to question. The whole idea of the long fifty-year swings during the nineteenth century simply must be abandoned. The great peaks and slumps in prices and employment produce a semblance of unified long periods which closer investigation shows to be a fiction. We are far from a full understanding of all the problems broached in this book. But this at least is clear: the sooner the 'Great Depression' is banished from the literature, the better.

Select Bibliography

THE following references cover the most important analytical work on the 'Great Depression', nearly all of it published since 1945. Contemporary material is excluded and so are purely theoretical studies and literature solely concerned with events in countries other than Britain. To keep the list reasonably short no references are given separately to books and articles dealing with particular industries or firms. Most of this work is surveyed in the first book in the bibliography, which also contains select bibliographies at the end of each chapter. Cross-references to other works in the list are shown in square brackets.

1   D. H. Aldcroft (ed.), *The Development of British Industry and Foreign Competition 1875–1914* (London, 1968). Various writers examine the experiences of the major British industries (except, oddly enough, shipbuilding). The quality is variable but it is essential reading for the period. There are useful bibliographies.

2   D. H. Aldcroft, 'The Entrepreneur and the British Economy 1870–1914', *Economic History Review*, 2nd ser., XVII (1964), takes the view that entrepreneurial weaknesses were at the root of Britain's industrial difficulties.

3   D. H. Aldcroft, 'Technical Progress and British Enterprise 1875–1914', *Business History*, VIII (1966). Another analysis of similar problems.

4   E. Ames and N. Rosenberg, 'Changing Technological Leadership and Industrial Growth', in *Economic Journal*, LXXIII (1963), discusses the early-start argument largely from a theoretical point of view.

5   W. Ashworth, *An Economic History of England 1870–1939* (1960). Apart from the assumption in the title that 'England' is equivalent to 'Great Britain', this is much the best general book on the period.

6   W. Ashworth, 'Changes in the Industrial Structure 1870–1914', *Yorkshire Bulletin of Economic and Social Research* (1965). This is one of seven articles in this special issue of the

journal entitled *Studies in the British Economy, 1870–1914,* ed. John Saville. See also [48].

7 W. Ashworth, 'The Late Victorian Economy', *Economica* (1966) discusses the productivity of capital and the calls being made upon it which were more and more of a relatively unproductive nature.

8 H. L. Beales, 'The Great Depression in Industry and Trade', *Economic History Review,* v (1934). This is the classic article casting doubt on older interpretations of the period which remained the last word on the subject for almost two decades.

9 A. K. Cairncross, *Home and Foreign Investment 1870–1913* (Cambridge, 1953). Though statistically out of date, a major study of the capital market and of fluctuations in investment at home and overseas.

10 D. J. Coppock, 'The Climacteric of the 1890s: A Critical Note', *Manchester School,* xxiv (1956), is a criticism of [38] and suggests that the turning-point in British economic growth should be brought forward to the 1870s at least.

11 D. J. Coppock, 'The Causes of the Great Depression, 1873–1896', *Manchester School,* xxix (1961). An essential article which stresses above all the impact of a falling rate of growth of industrial demand.

12 D. J. Coppock, 'Mr Saville on the Great Depression: A Reply', *Manchester School,* xxxi (1963) – a sharp and mainly convincing reply to [52].

13 D. J. Coppock, 'British Industrial Growth during the Great Depression: a Pessimist's View', *Economic History Review,* 2nd ser., xvii (1964). Another sharp and convincing reply, this time to Musson [35].

14 C. Erickson, *British Industrialists; Steel and Hosiery 1850–1950* (Cambridge, 1959), is a pioneering study into the origins and careers of businessmen in two well-contrasted industries.

15 C. H. Feinstein, 'Home and Foreign Investment. Some Aspects of Capital Formation and Finance in the U.K. 1870–1913'. This is an unpublished Ph.D. thesis, available only in Cambridge University Library, but a major study, improving on the statistics in [9] and developing fully the link between profits and home industrial investment.

16   T. W. Fletcher, 'The Great Depression of British Agriculture, 1873–1896', *Economic History Review*, 2nd ser., XIII (1961), stresses that the depression affected only certain sectors of agriculture whereas others prospered to a marked extent.

17   M. Frankel, 'Obsolescence and Technological Change in a Mature Economy', *American Economic Review*, XLV (1955), develops the idea of related costs in the context of the early-start argument.

18   H. J. Habakkuk, *American and British Technology in the 19th Century* (Cambridge, 1962). A difficult but brilliant theoretical and historical survey which places particular emphasis on relative factor costs.

19   R. P. Higonnet, 'Bank Deposits in the U.K., 1870–1914', *Quarterly Journal of Economics*, LXXI (1957), corrects the statistics in [37] and suggests that changes in the volume of money may indeed have influenced the price level.

20   W. Hoffmann, *British Industry 1700–1950* (Oxford, Blackwell, 1955). Source of the only complete index of industrial production for the period, open to considerable criticism in detail, but reflecting the main trends at the end of the nineteenth century accurately enough.

21   A. Imlah, *Economic Elements in the Pax Britannica* (Cambridge, Mass., 1958). Source for the only reasonable calculation of annual changes in British overseas investment in the nineteenth century and also for the terms of trade.

22   C. P. Kindleberger, *The Terms of Trade* (Technology Press, 1956), contains a most detailed and sophisticated treatment of relative price movements in the trade of European countries.

23   C. P. Kindleberger, *Economic Growth in France and Britain 1851–1950* (Cambridge, Mass., 1964). A historical study of remarkable penetration by an economist. Better on France than Britain, but containing a particularly fine chapter on technological change.

24   D. S. Landes, 'Technological Change and Development in Western Europe 1750–1914', in *Cambridge Economic History of Europe*, vol. VI, part 1 (Cambridge, 1966). A superb comparative study of comparative industrialisation in the nineteenth century. It over-emphasises the German successes and the British failures but is brilliantly provocative.

25   W. T. Layton and G. Crowther, *An Introduction to the Study of Prices* (1935). The interpretation is now very out of date but it contains much useful detail on individual price changes in Britain throughout the nineteenth century.

26   W. A. Lewis, 'World Production, Prices and Trade, 1870–1960', *Manchester School*, XX (1952), examines statistically the relationships between these three elements in world trade, and, in passing, casts considerable doubt on the validity of long-cycle analysis.

27   W. A. Lewis and P. J. O'Leary, 'Secular Swings in Production and Trade', *Manchester School*, XXIII (1955), examines the interaction of the twenty-year 'Kuznets' cycles in the U.S.A., Britain, France and Germany, and shows, surprisingly, how independent they were of each other.

28   W. Malenbaum, *The World Wheat Economy, 1885–1939* (Harvard, 1933). An excellent book, theoretical, statistical, technical and historical.

29   R. C. O. Matthews, *The Trade Cycle* (Cambridge, 1959). A largely theoretical outline, but with one section devoted to historical analysis of a most incisive character.

30   R. C. O. Matthews, 'Some Aspects of Post-War Growth in the British Economy in relation to Historical Experience', *Manchester Statistical Society Transactions* (1964). A very valuable article emphasising the interaction of twenty-year cycles of home and foreign investment.

31   G. Maynard, *Economic Development and the Price Level* (1962). A theoretical study of the relationship between prices and economic growth with sections on both British and American experience during the period.

32   G. M. Meier, 'Long-Period Determinants of Britain's Terms of Trade, 1880–1913', in *Review of Economic Studies*, XX (1952–3). An important article discussing several possible factors affecting prices and the terms of trade, including gold, and concentrating upon relative changes in productivity and the bargaining power of labour.

33   B. R. Mitchell and P. Deane, *Abstract of British Historical Statistics* (Cambridge, 1963).

34   A. E. Musson, 'The Great Depression in Britain, 1873–1896: a Reappraisal', *Journal of Economic History*, XIX (1959). A useful survey of the literature since Beales's article [8].

35 A. E. Musson, 'British Industrial Growth during the Great Depression (1873–96): Some Comments', *Economic History Review*, 2nd ser., xv (1963), and the same, 'A Balanced View', *Economic History Review*, 2nd ser., xvii (1964). These two articles form part of an argument, together with Coppock [13], over the extent and significance of the relative decline in British industrial growth.

36 J. Pedersen and O. S. Petersen, *An Analysis of Price Behaviour* (Copenhagen, 1938). A more up-to-date and comprehensive study than [25] and one based on European rather than simply British data.

37 J. T. Phinney, 'Gold Production and the Price Level', in *Quarterly Journal of Economics*, xlvii (1933). An influential article seeking to disprove a connection between prices and the quantity of money during the period but now super- seded by Higonnet [19].

38 E. H. Phelps Brown and S. J. Handfield-Jones, 'The Climac- teric of the 1890s: a Study in the Expanding Economy', *Oxford Economic Papers* (1952). This article first drew attention to the break in income per head during the 1890s, attributing it largely to the absence of new all-pervading innovations.

39 E. H. Phelps Brown and P. E. Hart, 'Share of Wages in the National Income', *Economic Journal*, lxii (1952), is important most of all for its statistical analysis and makes interesting points about the rise in real wages up to the end of the nineteenth century.

40 E. H. Phelps Brown and S. A. Ozga, 'Economic Growth and the Price Level', *Economic Journal*, lxv (1955). One of the earliest works to cast doubt on the role of supply in explain- ing movements in prices during the nineteenth and twentieth centuries.

41 A. W. Phillips, 'The Relation between Unemployment and the Rate of Change of Money Wage Rates in the U.K., 1861–1957', *Economica*, xxv (1958). A theoretical and statistical analysis of a difficult problem.

42 H. W. Richardson, 'Retardation in Britain's Industrial Growth 1870–1913', *Scottish Journal of Political Economy*, iix (1965), argues that the slow rate of growth resulted from a low rate of structural change partly at least because of a discontinuity in the flow of major innovations.

43 H. W. Richardson, 'Over-Commitment in Britain before 1930', *Oxford Economic Papers* (1965), applies similar ideas to a slightly longer period, taking particular account of the early-start argument.

44 D. H. Robertson, 'New Light on an Old Story', *Economica*, xv (1948). A penetrating review of Rostow [45].

45 W. W. Rostow, *The British Economy of the 19th Century* (Oxford, 1948). A pioneering work of the greatest significance which emphasises the importance of shifts in investment outlay in explaining nineteenth-century trends.

46 W. W. Rostow, 'The 'Historical Analysis of the Terms of Trade', *Economic History Review*, 2nd ser., IV (1951), discovers no simple cyclical pattern of behaviour for the terms of trade.

47 S. B. Saul, *Studies in British Overseas Trade 1870–1914* (Liverpool, 1960). Useful for factors influencing the rate of growth of exports and the incidence of fluctuations in world trade.

48 S. B. Saul, 'The Export Economy 1870–1914', *Yorkshire Bulletin of Economic and Social Research* (1965), adds further statistical material on overseas trade and suggests reasons for the slow growth of types of exports.

49 S. B. Saul, 'The Market and the Development of the Mechanical Engineering Industries in Britain, 1860–1914', *Economic History Review*, 2nd ser., XX (1967), stresses the continuing success of many branches of the engineering industry and suggests that market factors in part explain the weaknesses in other sectors.

50 J. Saville, 'Comments on Professor Rostow's *British Economy of the 19th Century*', in *Past and Present* (1954). A critical review of [45].

51 J. Saville, 'Some Retarding Factors in the British Economy before 1914', *Yorkshire Bulletin of Economic and Social Research*, XIII (1961). A short survey emphasising that the problem was in large measure one of developing new industrial sectors alongside the old which still remained highly profitable and progressive in many instances, a point of view subsequently elaborated in [43] and [49].

52 J. Saville, 'Mr. Coppock on the Great Depression: a Critical Note', *Manchester School*, XXXI (1963), criticises [11] for underestimating the role of costs and for exaggerating the

decelerating rate of growth of industrial demand in explaining the price-fall.

53 D. Ward, 'The Public Schools and Industry in Britain after 1870', *Journal of Contemporary History*, II (1967), argues that the new public schools created a pattern of education unsuited to the needs of industry without, however, being able to show how many sons of industrialists or future industrialists in fact attended such schools.

54 C. Wilson, 'Economy and Society in Late Victorian Britain', *Economic History Review*, 2nd ser., XVIII (1965), not very convincingly argues by example that British entrepreneurship was more capable than some have believed.

Addendum

Noel G. Butlin, 'A New Plea for the Separation of Ireland', *Journal of Economic History*, XXVIII (1968). It suggests that the rate of growth of G.N.P. in England, Wales and Scotland was significantly higher than that in the United Kingdom between 1860 and 1890, though the omission of Ireland probably makes little difference to the rate of change of industrial growth. Butlin points out too that, given the continuous stagnation in Irish growth, the growth rate for Great Britain must have declined more sharply in the quarter-century to 1914 than that for the whole United Kingdom.

D. N. McCloskey, 'Productivity Change in British Pig lron, 1870–1939', *Quarterly Journal of Economics*, LXXXII (1968), attempts to measure total productivity in the industry, relating output to the input of capital and labour. He comes to the conclusion that although productivity was stagnant from the late 1880s, it did not lag much behind that in the American industry before the First World War.

D. N. McCloskey, 'Did Victorian Britain Fail?', *Economic History Review*, 2nd series, XXIII (1970), looks again at measures of productivity and suggests that the sharp dip came after 1900.

D. N. McCloskey (ed.), *Essays on a Mature Economy: Britain after 1840* (London, 1971), contains a number of studies of the attitude of British entrepreneurs to technological change and concludes that in the main the slow response can be attributed to objective economic circumstances.

D. N. McCloskey and Lars Sandberg, 'From Damnation to Redemption: Judgments on the late Victorian Entrepreneur', *Explorations in Economic History*, IX (1971). Yet another general essay based largely on the book edited by McCloskey.

Index